Mosaic

Mosaic

A Collection of Poems

Iadalang Pyngrope

PARTRIDGE
A Penguin Random House Company

To order additional copies of this book, contact
Partridge India
000 800 10062 62
www.partridgepublishing.com/india
orders.india@partridgepublishing.com

Dedicated to my husband Mark and my children
Samanda, Arwanker and Dawankyrpang

Contents

Now . . .

Then . . . .

Songs

Preface

I have held on to these poems for a long time. I have read them to family and friends and now the time has come to share them with the world.

Poems in the *NOW* Section were written fairly recently. Those in the *THEN* Section were composed years ago.

9th November 2013

Iadalang Pyngrope

Now . . .

I told my friends

I told my friends
'The Muse is dead'
For good or for bad
There seems to be a resurrection of sorts
This Lenten season
I muse as I patiently wait for my son;
What better place to introspect
Than the hallowed grounds of St. Edmund's
Pine-lined and fenced
Like the thoughts I pen.

Tribute to Thomas Jones

On a warm winter morning, in Kolkata
We embarked on a pilgrimage
The children obedient but bewildered
Asking what on earth were we doing
Spending Christmas day trudging along shabby
    streets,
No malls to look at, no fancy cars,
Nothing particularly interesting,
Except for a welcome distraction
A puppy given a bath on the roadside.

I thought of the festival madness of Shillong
The cakes, choirs and concerts
The latest fashion, flaunted in church aisles,
Frantic shoppers, ready to pay just a little bit more
For the perfect match.
It was rather strange to leave all that behind,
For a walk along Karaya Street
In unfamiliar environs:
We came upon it rather suddenly
Behind huge locked iron gates,

We rapped on the gate and a hello later
Walked into the graveyard overgrown with weeds
Tombstones cracked, broken crosses strewn all
    over,
I half expected a Magwitch to jump up chains
    clanging,
The lady-in-charge chatted amicably
'Occasionally a few Khasis visit Pastor Jones'
We were silent, overwhelmed by the moment . . .

Advancing, we saw it—white marble
Well kept, his tomb,
'Pioneer, Forerunner, Father of the Khasi
    Alphabet'.
Standing there, I spoke to him
You sailed on rough seas for five months to
    reach us,
You lost family and endured,
Misunderstood and ahead of your times
You finally sought refuge here in the city,

As you lay dying, what memories crossed your
    mind?
The verdant Khasi Hills, the fresh air of the
    mountains,
The unforgiving, relentless rain,
Or the wafting of hymns in the country side
Of your beloved Wales.
You must have felt lonely, forgotten then,
Now rendered worthy, your memory lives on
In the hills you left behind
Once upon a time.

*This poem is based on a visit to Scottish Church Cemetery,
Kolkata, the burial place of Thomas Jones (1810-1849),
Welsh Missionary to the Khasi Hills, Meghalaya, India.*

My city

From my terrace, I look at my City
Ten thousand lights blink back at me
The darkness hiding the unsavoury:
Next morning I drive through the ugliness
I write a requiem in my head
A few places have magically retained serenity,
I carefully store the view in my memory
To be re-viewed when those places
No longer exist

I am haunted by buildings
Grotesque and monstrous, the face of
    modernity,
I am haunted by over-populated junctions,
And hawkers that leave a mountain of rubbish
    after them
I am haunted by dirty plastic-clogged drains
Where streams once flowed
I am haunted by a people incorrigible
Bartering their identity for thirty pieces of silver,
I am haunted by a thousand terrors
Of what my City will be-when I am old,
When my children inherit it, or what's left of it.

Reminiscence I

Life is complicated now
The dilapidated building across the street
Sold for one and a half crores
The new owners stated matter-of-factly
That the earth in their village had turned black,
The waters had dried up and grass had
Turned into thin wisps on a bald pate:
Back then in the old times, they were poor yet rich,
Fresh flowing rivers, clothed in a mantle of
    green on both sides.

Life is complicated now
Too many choices make a heady mix
Back in the old days
It was either Ambassador or Premier
Maybe a rattling jeep and a decent
Forty kilometers per hour.
Today you do twenty in a Swift
Pedestrians walk on drain edges
Because we love our cars too much!

Life is complicated now

Even Christianity has not been spared

Choose your denomination from the hundred
    available locally.

Or better still, start your own

There's room for everyone.

Life is complicated now.

In cyber-age, policemen are busy arresting

Black magic practitioners, lynch mobs and their ilk,

And everywhere a renewed interest in the
rather choosy serpent spirit

That consumes only 'us'.

Back then, serpent notwithstanding,

Policemen at the Beat House next door,

Occasionally flogged thieves,

Also hosted snake charmers, Bihu dancers and
    monkeys too,

While urchins watched wide-eyed.

Life is complicated now
School children totter under over-sized school
   bags
Training to be porters on the side.
Back then we learnt more with a lot less
Found time to play and dirty our knees
With our favourite mongrel wagging his tail
Behind a wicket gate
That remained unlocked the whole night
   through.

Reminiscence II

My childhood replete with memories
Of picture frames on walls
Their Majesties, resplendent, a ruler's gaze
Adorning living rooms long after independence.

Mother spoke of eating giant rasgollas,
To celebrate the first independence day,
Distributed by a prominent citizen, of course,
Father and friends sang the national anthem
In Lady Hydari Park, stumbling a little,
It was difficult, you see, after years
Of "God save our gracious Queen".

Those picture frames of the Broad and Narrow
    way,
Tiny figures crowding, making their way up,
I felt sorry for those destined for hell
Having chosen the easy path
I scrutinized them intently-half wishing
They could change direction
But it was not to be!

You will recall,

In Christian homes, invariably

"Christ is the head of this house

 . . . . The silent listener to every conversation'

It always left me apprehensive

Of the eavesdropper who knew everything

Including the fact that we grabbed left-over biscuits

On our way to the kitchen, after guests left.

You will recall

Glittering brass over the mantelpiece,

Lovingly polished every Saturday

Of cozy rooms that spoke comfort

Inviting you to a blazing fireplace

That warmed you to the core,

As you listened to BBC, Radio Rangoon

And sometimes Radio Ceylon—

Not forgetting the delectable request
    programme of AIR Shillong,

You will recall, the simplicity of it all.

Birds in my Garden

There are many birds in my garden
Blue-flecked, black and white,
Sea green and an unbelievably bright orange,
As a child I wondered!
Where did God get that dye from?
Possibly a dash of turmeric with a pinch of
    sunset.

The boring brown sparrow green with envy
    flies around them
Pretending not to care,
The crow that sips water
From overhanging eaves, caws contentedly
-like a Khasi crow,
(the ones in the plains are cacophonous)

The orange flock has not been seen of late
For who could ignore them against the
    background of pine,
This morning the crow woke me up
Cawing soulfully,
I looked out and saw him
Atop the Airtel tower
I thought he looked sad.

The Buffet

Supposed to be sophisticated, modern
This waiting, plate in hand, as if for alms,
As the person ten places ahead decides
    between this rice and that,
Look around and note with satisfaction
A friend ten places behind and another,
One shuffle at a time—a milestone is reached
The plates!
Pile them on, a bewildering assortment of
    Indian, Chinese and Indigenous,
(Because no second helpings are possible)
Destined to eat standing, you hold your plate,

Clutch your purse, fearful of unintended nudges,
That could stain your silk permanently,
You smile and nod, pretending everything is fine,
Your fingers ache; your feet are killing you
In the high heels you bought the day before,
Chewing mindlessly, you stare, seeing, yet not
    seeing,

Where did your appetite go?
It died, somewhere along the way.

The Rape of the Lock
(WITH DUE APOLOGY TO ALEXANDER POPE)

'For, lo, thou shalt conceive, and bear a son'
The woman heard the words and knew her son
    was special,
But-did she know about the lion, three hundred
    foxes?
Exploits, too numerous to name.

He loved Delilah-yet not trusting her enough.

He held on to his secret

Each time she cried 'the Philistines be upon thee'

He jumped up, broke loose and made mockery of them

Thrice was she lied to, until one day

She coaxed the secret out of his soul,

Deceptive smile intact, she planned his fall,

Alas! While sleeping on her knees

He lost his locks, his strength drained

He stood on his feet, feeble

Knowing at last that the Lord had departed from him.

They led him away, easily

Delilah, triumphant, flush with praise from the
    Philistines,

Strode like a Queen.

Later-when she saw Samson in fetters

Eyes gouged out, bereft of everything

Did she regret the rape of the lock?

Some residue of affection spoke silently,
    perhaps

Or was she simply being patriotic?

They dragged him to the temple
To be entertained,
Blind Samson felt the thousands stare,
With one last prayer, an inhuman summoning of
    strength,
He pushed the pillars; they submitted, gave way,
The temple trembled, cracked and crumbled
Upon the Philistines-burying Samson too:
And Delilah? Perhaps, watching . . . .
From behind a pillar she agonized, tormented
Until a huge stone hit her and she fell

In a swirl of dust, crying out his name.

Did she survive to live a nightmare?

Seeing Samson again and again with the locks
at her feet?

You will agree with me

You will agree with me
When I say-I fail to understand
The patience of Job
To have everything taken away
Given only festering skin and scabs
Taunted by friend and spouse
Made miserable
All because someone was trying to prove a point.

You will agree with me
When I say-I fail to understand
The predicament of the elder brother
Dutiful, obedient, largely ignored:
The prodigal, squanderer of inheritance
Returned to a grand reception
And a brother sulking in the wings.

You will agree with me
When I say-I fail to understand
Equal wages for a whole day's work
And for those who labour
For an hour only before closing time
Strange sense of justice!
Wouldn't you say?

You will agree with me
When I say-the human mind
Cannot comprehend a magnanimity
That is God's alone
When I understand his love for me
Then only, can I fathom his love for others
Whether I understand Job or not
What mattered was that he understood God.

On being a poet

I owe a lot to traffic jams
I think my thoughts out while to and fro from work
Or ferrying my brood to school and tuition
But the overall question remains
Why do I write?
To give my ideas, words
And words—wings,
I want my words to grasp you by the throat,
To make you jump out of your skin,
To shake you out of your slumber

To whisper in the quietness of the night
To echo in your mind as you sit in a doctor's
    waiting room
To provoke, never indifference.

When do you know you have arrived?
Is it when you have won a something or the
    other prize?
Or when a research scholar asks you
Why have you put a comma here, a colon there?
You write because you have to

You cannot always explain a figure of
  speech . . . .
You never knew you were writing one
Until they told you.

Ode to Malala

Malala, they called you the bravest girl in the
    world,
Who could have imagined
That a ride on a school bus in Swat
Could take you to Birmingham
Leaving you to count your blessings
In a strange country, far away from home

The world watched you, wondering
How you could smile still
While we, with nondescript burdens
Walk about, selfish, lusting for the irrelevant,
You are fighting for all of us
But the tragedy is we do not know it
Secure in our little worlds
We would have to live again a hundred times
To be as brave as you are

Then . . . . .

Roing (1992)

Nestled lovingly by snow-capped peaks
Your wide expanses stretch,
Beckoning like a lover
Cradling the merry-making
In your lap, you glowed,
Echoing mountains, sharing
Jealously guarding
The sanctity that is yours.

You who are undefiled
Will you be prostituted
When ribbons are cut and lamps lighted
Sucked dry, your rivers will
Bare their breasts to the sun,
Your skin pock-marked with a thousand slums
No tresses to shield,
Only tiny wisps fluttering helplessly
And sterility sets in

With only memories
Edged deep in the wrinkles of men
Of a time
When effortlessly you had won us
We of different climes.

This poem is based on a visit to Roing, a town in Arunachal Pradesh, India in 1992.

What if it does?

We often say it cannot happen to me,
What if it does, What do I do?
Do I stand numb, palsied by the shock of it all
Or do I mumble incoherently muttering words I
    do not hear;
Perhaps I will make a supreme effort to control
    mind and body,
If then my questioning will be calm
While my throbbing heart indignantly agitates
    against the encaging,
But will I still quote, "God's in his heaven . . . ."

You never know, I may just faint . . . . Sweet
    temporary oblivion
Only to wake up and find the same world,
There is always the possibility of a 'massive
    heart attack' and subsequent death.

Am I being theatrical?
I don't know about that but I will not be an
    extremist
What then of the remnants of my life, my flaky
    life
Do I paste the crumbling shreds together

And muse over the all-too-obvious ugly joints,
I may mourn of happier days and live in the ago,
I may live in the present with a vengeance
With a sardonic twist to my mouth
That makes the optimist's brain imperceptibly
    shrink in size
Compressed to a realization
Like a fruit shrivelling and dried in the sun,
Deprived of something and bestowed with
    something else.

I may talk and sermonize,

Lecture inevitably soliloquize,

They will call me names I don't understand,

Can I dare push it all to the back of my mind and
restore it to virgin territory

As if I was born yesterday, ready for the picks
and the shovels

For the ideas and impressions scrambling in and
out,

Clearing the overgrowth and undergrowth,

The sowing, weeding, fertilizing, harvesting,

Perhaps the ancient process can take place
again;

But I can almost hear the jerks, creaks, the
   wheel slowly turning stopping
A jerk, a creak
And then another one, with a sigh in between.
Oh! All this heavy pondering makes me feel
   miserable and more,
I will pray that it does not happen.
But what if it does, what do I do?
Do I . . . .

They said long ago

They said long ago 'this is the place'
And planted neat bungalows with prim hedges
Over which dusky faces peered
At the Mem and the Sahib
Sipping their evening tea.
Today, barbed wire and high walls
Shelter the same faces
From their own kinsmen
For 'insecurity' reasons.

They said long ago 'this is the Scotland of the East'
Rolling hills and transparent waters
That wash lush banks,
Pine scented air and flaming orchids
'Shall we go up for the summer', they said
Today, baited by that phrase
The unsuspecting tourist is assaulted
With a cacophony of rock shows, and mainland
    music

Incongruously labelled 'Autumn Festival'
And the tourist from the Metro
'Why I've seen it all before'
And no one listens when he says
'Could I have some more Cherra please'.

They said long ago 'these are the people
Shall we study their matrilineal system' they
    said.
And scholars smelling fresh hunting grounds
    came

To churn out PhD's and scholastic reputations
And we were astounded at our own difference
Today, a few good men cry 'Men's lib;
And women busy themselves
With a new branch of the Women's Commission
To raise the status of Women, They say;
And the sociologist is confounded,
As he pretends to understand
Nevertheless
To impress
He adds a new chapter 'Emerging new trends.'

They said long ago 'let us settle and do business
    here,
Warm, hospitable' people and
Endless avenues to lead to prosperity
Today, they say apprehensive stares have
    replaced the smiles
And they claim to have diagnosed the disease
Fear Psychosis alas!

But wouldn't you suffer from this malady

If you also belonged to a people who comprise

A grain of rice

In a bagful of India

A grain that could simply slither away

And be forgotten

Because they did not know it existed in the first
place.

Insight

You told me the truth, an unwelcome truth,
Yes, I am-I am mad;
It was terrifying and spine-chilling at the
    beginning,
Now that what is reason to you is exhausted,
    crippled and invalidated
I am happily mad;
My world is beautiful and assuring,

My imagination opens, crackles like pine-cones
    in the sun
I shed my skin of hypocritical 'normal behaviour'
But what is that again?
We were talking of my destabilized mind,
Well, my friend, my supposed madness throws
    a crazy enlightenment,

It tells me YOU are mad,

You categorize us-you dull-deadening thing;

Ah! It is a pity but your expression tells me I am
   right.

Change

The soft, rounded tops of pine-clustered hills,
Cool, clear, sparkling waters and gushing
abundance
Of nature; Life surrounds and I am contented.
The soothing touch of the sun caresses the
outspread surface
Constructing a thousand-mirrored images
gleaming and glinting,
Losing definition just a moment after, giving
way to others;

Melodies effusive-soft, subtle, loud and assertive,
I shut my eyes and savour every bit of it.
Years later,
Longing, eagerness to soak in that experience,
The drone of machinery has usurped the
    ethereal tones,
The outline of hills distorted by evil black pipes
    changing the hue of the sky
I turn away sadly.

Crossroads

Among tiny shreds of Lawrence and Drayton
Cups of tea and suppositions
Thoughts take shape,
Deliberately confused
Well-defined streaks of paint maliciously smudged.
Yet they deny subjugation

The flicker of one sensitivity quickens another
Like two embers burning together,
Burning themselves out into an anti-climax
The ashes then assume significance a hand-me-
    down importance,
There's something tragic about them
Like everything else that is second best

A meeting at a crossroad cold assessments
But . . .
Soon the hazy blur of human traffic
Discriminated and set some apart

Now another crossroad ahead
Clear destinations and signposts
I slow down my steps
It is not foolishness, I know
'A human weakness', they say ultimately,
Only a few comprehend
You do, and this is my token to you.

Place and Time

(A translation of the Khasi poem "*KA JAKA BAD KA POR*" written by W.R. Laitflang published in the collection '*Ki Myllung Khasi*' (1980)).

In the same place, sweat trickles
In the same place, bodies bleed,
In the same place, carcasses rot
In the same place, weeds thrive
Only the time differs.

In the same place, stones stand
In the same place, trees crash
In the same place, fire corrodes
In the same place, water erodes
Only the time differs.

In the same place, hills thrust,
In the same place, forests surge,
In the same place, streams flow,
In the same place, they are swallowed,
Only the time differs.

In the same place, beasts roam
In the same place, machines drone
In the same place, cromlechs fed
In the same place, houses are erected
Only the time differs.

In the same place, waters submerge
In the same place, deserts emerge
In the same place, fish abound
In the same place, rocky mounds
Only the time differs.

In the same place, cities sprawl
In the same place, Jackals call
In the same place, soldiers fall
In the same place, vanishes all,
Only the time differs.

At the same time, things burgeon and flourish
At the same time, things shrivel and perish
At the same time, things breathe and quicken
At the same time, things cease and stiffen
Only the place differs.

Shredded Thoughts

When the man on the street
Declares that honesty is not the best policy
Strange diseases eat the insides
While the outside is rejuvenated pathetically.
And the mind, a confused heap of perceptions
Seeking for the comfortable
For the truth is not always so
When morality becomes archaic so,
Gazed at with wonder—a fossil in a museum
Ah! When our bank accounts swell
While our bodies dwindle into shrivelled remnants

And our last breath throttled by visions of
    accumulated wealth
And a voice up there says,
'How foolish they were to think themselves
    immortal!'

Published in Dancing in Light (2002), part of the Letters
from the Soul series by the International Library of Poetry,
Owing Mills, MD 21117, U.S.A

Why read my book

Indeed, why read my book,
Books are meant to be read
But some are destined to be merely
Looked at, fingered rather carelessly
And tossed aside

And so, why read mine?

I am no Phoolan Devi, No Mahasweta

No scandalizing Shobha

Only a 'working' woman

Bothered by the price of a kg of sugar and no, not
blue mangoes

Planning the evening dinner for years together

And merrily packing lunchboxes in the morning

If I made outrageous statements
About outrageous issues, you would sit up,
But I am no Member of Parliament,
No Padma Shri, no President of an N.G.O.
There is no unearthing of a scam
No dams to damn
Only sometimes, doors (my own) to slam.

Shall I grow bold, shall I grow bold?

Shall I wear the bottoms of my 'jainsem'.

Unhemmed, unembroidered

By whirring machines in the night

I do not know because in this world

You misplace a word and you have an 'ism'
pointing at you.

Forgive me, for simply telling.

The Trucks

Those monsters with colourful behinds,
Screaming headlines!
Accidents that throw the blame on drunken
    drivers,
Monster trucks that race through the night
Rash youngsters on bikes that meander madly
Mostly—the trucks are targeted
Polluting our highways in more ways than one
They obstruct 'smooth flow of traffic'?
But we forget
They bring us our daily bread.

Can We Walk A Straight Line

Can we walk a straight line?
That is the question I am asked often
I cannot say
The alluring thirst-quenchers on the highway
    suggest we cannot
It is evident, we love the zig zag
Those stop-you-dead-in-your-tracks names
Can kill you softly with their songs
I love the creativity of the signboards above the
    shops
Not after four anthologies of poetry
Could I ever come up with words of import
Such as these

Dilemma

There are no shortcuts to heaven
Only the route you must take
Hewn with rough stones
That cut your feet, bleeding red
Elysium sounds an easier proposition
But even the ancient Greeks had to apply
    themselves
To win the prize
The other day, I was told
The criminal on the cross
Secured what seemed a shortcut to heaven
Someone remarked
You have to be really bad or really good to get
    to Heaven!

Songs

Song of Assurance

"I will lift up mine eyes unto the hills, from whence cometh help" (Psalm 121:1)

1. When lonely in pride, I think not of God;
    When troubles engulf me, in storms I am caught;
    When counsel of friends, in vain I have sought;
    Where shall my refuge be?

Chorus   I lift up my eyes to the hills,

My hungry soul he fulfils

My burden he knows, my plea he
has heard,

The Lord who made heaven and
earth;

My soul from its bondage to free

New courage he gives to me;

He sheds His Light to dispel the
night

Forever my refuge He'll be

2. When weakened with sorrow, I struggle to fight;
   When tempted by Satan and wrong becomes right;
   When darkened with sin, my life knows no light;
   Where shall my refuge be?

3. When bleak seems my future, and cloudy
   the sky;
   When hopes have been dashed, born only to
   die;
   When life has no purpose and joys pass me
   by
   Where shall my refuge be?

Note: *This poem has been set to music, translated into Khasi and sung on several occasions.*

We Sing Joyfully

There's a new day dawning
New challenges we see
But together we can conquer
Victorious we shall be.
There are paths we must walk
And rivers we must cross
Hand in hand we'll make our journey
As we sing joyfully.

Chorus:

It's a warm welcome to you

It's a warm welcome to you

It's a moment we shall cherish

And happy greetings too.

Our hearts all resounding, our voices

proclaim

That we're honoured by your presence

So welcome, once again.

Summits may look distant
But one step at a time
Your helping hand to guide us
No mountain hard to climb.
Let us look for silver
In the darkest cloud
God will lead us, ne'er forsake us
There's hope without a doubt.

Farewell song

1. The tide of time is rolling
   The parting hour is near
   With heavy hearts we gather
   With friends from far and near
   It's time to bid you farewell
   It's not easy as you can see
   But God's plan has its seasons
   To be lived accordingly

Chorus:

> Swiftly the days go by
> And with the grace of God on high
> We labour on, our burdens share
> Our faith in God and our hearts in prayer
> We'll trust in his loving care.

2. A long long way you've travelled
   The days have come and gone
   The memories that surround us
   Are fresh as summer's morn
   The times we spent together
   In sun and storm and shade
   We cannot but remember
   The joys will never fade.

3. The service you have rendered
   Its value will remind
   The noble work and toiling
   Are footprints you leave behind
   Though parting brings us sorrow
   Yet that's the way it is
   But one thing we assure you
   Your presence we will miss.